WW2 Stories From The Little Red School-House

Dana Woodard

Written and Published in Canada

Printed in the USA

Copyright © 2017 Dana Woodard

ISBN: 0-9938776-2-1
ISBN-13: 978-0-9938776-2-9

DEDICATION

This book is dedicated to my whole family in Canada, in the U.S.A., and in Denmark. To those who loved Farmor and to those who loved to visit the Little Red School-House.

Will you love me when I am 101?

At the end of one of their week long stays at the Little Red School-House, Heather and Dana were saying their good-byes. Dana said "Good-bye Farmor! I love you!" Vera then asked "Will you love me when I am 90?" And Dana replied "Yes, I will love you even when you are 100." Vera then asked, "Will you love me when I am 101?" to which Dana replied with a chuckle "I will think about it." - age 9

I thought about it Farmor and I will love you when you are 101 and I will love you forever. - Dana

CONTENTS

1. EVERY STORY HAS A BEGINNING

"Oh gee, I want to be In that little red school house! " - old song

Every family has one. Or at least I like to think that they do. That one special home or cottage that has been around for years or perhaps decades and is a central gathering place for all the family members who come from far and wide to celebrate those special times like Thanksgiving, Christmas, and birthdays.

It's usually where a grandparent, parent or favourite aunt or uncle resides. It's the place that holds many precious memories and plenty of laughter and stories. The place where you couldn't imagine these gatherings taking place anywhere else. For our family it was "The Little Red School-House", as we affectionately called it. It was the home of our grandparents Vera and Ivan Jorgensen; two Danish immigrants who bought the place for a song when the township of Meyersberg auctioned it off decades ago. Vera and Ivan, who were better known as Farmor and Farfar (meaning "father's mother" and "father's father" in Danish) by my cousins and siblings and I, had taken the school house and renovated it to make it into a darling little home to call their own. While it had transitioned from what was once a community place of learning and gathering to one of a personal and family gathering place, it still retained many of the old school's unique and charming characteristics.

Our "Little Red School-House" was just that; a red brick school house built in 1901, complete with a white picket fence, wide cement stairs leading up to two big antiquated wooden doors and an actual working bell on a rope up in the bell tower. As kids, we often begged to ring the bell that could be heard all over the country side for miles around. As we got older we didn't ask to ring it any more because we knew that all the neighbours now regarded it as the S.O.S. bell. They knew that if they heard the bell ringing it was the signal to come running quick because something was wrong. Even if the phone lines were dead there was still a way to signal for help. It gave our family members a sense of comfort to know that although the closest of us lived hours away, the wonderful neighbours were always keeping an eye on the place and on the well being of those who lived inside.

Every room of the school house was filled with various things that piqued a child's curiosity. There was the little elf (or Nisser as it is called in Danish) sitting on the bathroom shelf. There was the radio room with cupboards filled with games and stuffed animals. In the spare bedroom there was a big red ceramic strawberry filled to the brim with pennies. Everytime we visited we were allowed to reach into the ceramic strawberry and grab a fist full of pennies, as many as one hand could hold, to take home with us. There was the wooden monkey hanging from the kitchen entrance way. Along side the monkey was a string of bells that we routinely rang just before every meal to call everyone to the dinner table. The entrance was filled with a collection of buttons hanging on the wall that Farmor and Farfar had collected on all of their trips all over Canada. The buttons said things like "I love milk" and " Let's Do

It! Travel Alberta". If you went into the coat room and looked way up high you could see a small trap door leading into the attic. No one ever went up there and who knows if there was even anything to see up there. I imagined it might be filled with things like you see in the movies. Maybe some creepy old dolls or rocking chairs or something. Most likely though there was nothing up there because it was much too difficult to get a ladder long enough to reach the trap door. In the same room was a trap door in the floor with a set of wooden stairs that was so well used that the steps had been worn down into smooth indents in the wood where people walked. My imagination of the history of the stairs alone was intriguing. How often do you see a set of stairs where the wood has been worn right down into grooves? As for the celler itself, we were fascinated by the old cabinets and books and toys down there, but it was dark and scary. So we tended to bring our treasures up from the cellar to the yard where we could play in the sunshine rather than confront our fears of spiders and maybe even ghosts.

The Little Red School-House was about a six hour drive from where we lived so we did not get to visit very often; maybe only once or twice a year on average. It was the highlight of my summers as a kid to be allowed to stay for a week or so with one of my younger sisters. Although the visits never seemed long enough, it was enough time to either get to hear a new story or to make up one of our own.

Stories were everywhere in this place. They were brought to us over BBQ's and games of croquet played over the sprawling lawn when all the cousins came together to visit. Stories were in the latest gossip from the neighbours; who told us who got that new job, or new car, or who was having a new grandchild. And they were in our imaginations. From imagining we were cowboys and pretending to shoot at the the cars that drove by from our tree fort in the front yard using the very same toy cowboy guns that my dad and uncle played with when they were kids, to the stories we made up of what might be lurking in the creepy old cellar. The ceilings in the house were about twelve feet high and there were cabinets in some rooms that went almost up to the full twelve feet. When you are only a child that twelve feet looks even taller than it does when you are grown up, so it sometimes felt like being in a giant's house.

The best stories though, were the ones that my Farmor made up in her head. You see, she was a child at heart and had just as active an imagination as we did. From a very young age my sister and I would sneak out of bed in the middle of the night and crawl into bed with Farmor, one of us on each side of her, giggling and telling jokes and making up stories. We would pull the covers up over our heads like a tent and and were careful to whisper so as not to wake up Farfar across the room in the other bed. We were entertained with tales of rainbow coloured ghosts in old mansions, pirates on ships, and lively limericks until we drifted off to sleep one by one.

Every story has a beginning and these stories begin across the ocean in a whole other country.

2. SCHOOL IN MORS, DENMARK

In the words of Vera as told to her son Willy

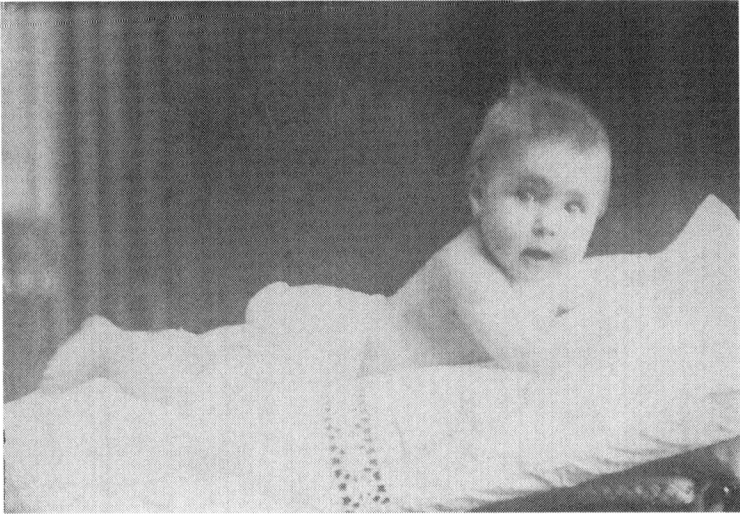

Vera age 18 months

The year I was born (1918) was the last year of the First World War. It was also the year that had the Spanish Flu epidemic and many, many people died. The country of Denmark and the whole of Europe was very run down from the aftermath of the big war and there were many things you could not buy. You could not even buy necessities for a long time.

When I lived in Mors, (that was an island) at first we couldn't get off the island unless we went on a ferry. Later on they built a bridge. We had a little two room school-house where we would go from age 7 to 10 in one room and age 11 to 14 in the next room. And that was what most of our education was like. There was no extra special education except kids school. But later on I took a little high school.

Vera 's father, Niels, the mailman

My father was a mailman and we lived on a small farm. There were six children and I was number five of the six. We were, as soon as we could, put to help with the work on the farm. As my father got older I would help him deliver the mail. He had 32 kilometers of area to cover and we either had to walk or use a bicycle. We were not allowed to use a horse and carriage because they could run away with the mail. So even in the winter he would have to walk. Very often he would take one of his children with him to help. When I was old enough, it was my turn and I would get half of the mail route for myself to deliver.

Raised Up Right

My father was very lenient with us kids, mostly because he was hardly ever home. He would start each day at 5 o'clock every morning. He spent most of his time out delivering the mail and when he came home he was out working on the farm. And then of course by the time he got home he would be tired so he would take a snooze.

My mom would look after the house and the garden and she was the one who had to look after bringing up the kids the right way. So whenever we did something wrong she would give us a rap or send us to bed or something. We didn't get away with it, that's for sure. Except maybe once...

One time the school teacher was reading aloud from a book. The story was about some people called "Molbos" (named after a certain place that they lived). The story went like this: "A big air balloon came over that little town and everyone in that Mol town

12

got very ,very scared because they didn't know what it was. So they all ran into the church and closed the doors. After awhile two of the bravest men climbed up to the top of the church tower to see if the monster was still floating over the town. Once they got to the top of the church tower they could see it because now they were up high. One man said to the other ' I think it's the devil himself!' The other man said 'No, I am certain by Satan it is not Satan because he hasn't got any horns on his forehead. Which translated to Danish is "Det er fanden ikke fanden for han har ingen horn i panden".

The first 'fanden' is considered swearing, however, for really religious people any mention of 'fanden' is swearing. After the school teacher read that book and said these words that we were not supposed to say, my sister Gerda and I thought it was so funny. So we would go around repeating it to each other and to my older brother Robert. Every time we could, and when we thought we were alone we would say " Det er fanden ikke fanden for han har ingen horn i panden" in a sing song fashion. One thing we forgot though was that my younger brother Herman, who was not in school yet because he was too young, was listening to us. For the longest time he didn't say anything. But then one day right in the middle of supper time he broke out into the sing song of "Det er fanden ikke fanden for han har ingen horn i panden!" at the table. My mom grabbed up the poor kid right from his supper, spanked his bum and put him into bed. Gerda, Robert and I never confessed that it was all our fault.

First Dog

When I was young I always wanted a dog. I loved dogs so much and begged and begged my mother and father to get me dog but they always said "No". One day I went to the birthday party of one of the kids on a farm a few miles away. Their dog had recently had a litter of puppies that were now ready to leave their mother. I spent the entire party playing with those puppies and all but ignoring the other kids.

When it was time to go home I was relentless at begging my mom and dad to let me take home one of those puppies. Finally my dad gave in and let me have one of the puppies. I was so happy! We went everywhere together.

But then one day my worst nightmare happened. My dog got

loose and wandered into a neighbours farm and the farmer shot him dead. The farmer said that my dog had been getting into his chicken coop for the past week. But that was the first time he had gotten away so I knew that this was a lie. I was inconsolable. I cried and I cried. I was so upset that my mom and dad never let me have another dog again because they were worried about how I would be if anything were to happen to another dog if I ever got one.

The Dead Chick

I remember as a child we had some chickens and some baby chicks. One of the chicks was a bit of a runt and one day it died. I was just young and I asked if I could play with the dead chick before they got rid of it. Surprisingly, I was allowed to play with it. I pretended the little dead chick was a doll. I held the little chick by the wings and gently bounced it up and down to make it look like the chick was dancing. Then I moved the wings back and forth like it was swimming. I had a good time playing with this little dead chick for quite a few minutes. Then all of a sudden, to my surprise, the little chick came back to life! I guess all the movement of it's wings had restarted the chick's heart. The chick was fine after that and grew up to be a healthy chicken.

Vera and Robert

Going To School With Robert

When my brother, Robert, was 6 years old he was very, very sick. He was in the hospital for three months. He had operations and at that time they did not have antibiotics. The doctor actually told my parents that they might not ever get him home. But he overcame it and he eventually did come home.

When he was seven he eventually had to go to school but he was still not very well. The kids in school would tease him because he couldn't keep up to what the other boys were doing. He couldn't run, he couldn't play ball and they called him a sissy. It got to the point where he no longer wanted to go to school. He would complain and say "Mom, I don't want to go to school".

My parents went and talked to the teacher about it and between them they decided that it might be a good idea to send me along with him to school for about a month to see if that would help.

Vera is the girl in the middle with the white bow in her hair

So away I went to school with my older brother. I remember the very first day I was there. The bigger boys who were teasing my brother called me over. They said "Vera, come over here. We want to talk to you." I was shy and scared. So they held out a candy and said "Here! We will give you a candy if you will come and talk to us." I couldn't resist. I went over there and they gave me the candy. Then they said "We will give you another one if you kiss Peter Havel. And you don't have to worry about it. We will catch him. And if he gets mad at you then we will help you." I stood there and didn't know what to think. "Do you want another candy?" they asked. "Yeah" I said. "Well, all you have to do ...we will catch him. You will kiss him. So...?" I said nothing. Then they said "We won't tease you and we won't tease your brother either." That did the trick. I knew that I was at school because they were teasing my brother. So I went and kissed Peter Havel. Poor Peter Havel. He was the one that got caught and got kissed and they started teasing Peter instead. They never teased Robert again.

Vera age 16 years

High School

Once I became a teenager, I had a lot of responsibilities given to me.

My mother , at the age of 42, had a baby, Nancy, who died. Nancy was only 24 hours old. I was the only girl still living at home at that time. My sisters were out working. In between me doing the washing and the cooking and the gardening and looking after the cows and everything, I helped my mother.

Eventually I was sent out to work with some of the local farmers. I did outdoor work and indoor work. I worked out in the fields with the men. There were big fields where we had to hoe turnips. I also worked with the women doing cooking and cleaning. So it was a busy life. Things were going well until one day a new problem arose.

My brother started to drink. I knew about it but I didn't tell my parents. By this time my eldest sister, Martine, was married and they had a little farm. One day she had scrubbed her kitchen floor and varnished it. That same day my brother had been drinking and he had also been fishing and had caught some flounders. That evening he filled up a basket with the flounders and decided to take them to Martine's house. There was no one in the kitchen since she had just finished varnishing the floor. He walked in on it and slipped and fell. He dropped the basket and the flounders fell all over the floor. Martine came in and boy was she mad. She went straight over and told my parents what my brother had done and that he was drunk when he did it. Oh, oh!

Now they wanted to do something about him. So they asked him to go to a different place where he had different friends because they felt that he had bad friends on the island of Mors. He didn't want to go. There was a Baptist high school on an island that was quite far away from us. It was a nice school and they wanted to send him there. But he refused. So they came to me and asked "Would you try to talk him into it? Would you go with him?" So I got after him and I talked and talked to him about it. Finally he did go, and that moved me away from the island I was born on and over to Sjaelland. So now I began my new life. I got into the high school courses and I liked it. The people there were very nice. We bicycled a lot and we had lots of friends. Both of us had a good time over there.

After my course was over I stayed an additional year to work there. I worked in the dining room, serving food for the students. I met two men there. One was Ivan. He was a student and he was trying to get his education because he wanted to go to Africa to be a missionary. He would eat in the kitchen with us because he did some work for the principal in the garden in between his studies. The other boy I liked was Sigurd. He was there because he wanted to be an officer in the military; a soldier. He needed some more education for that. The two of them both liked me also. But I chose Sigurd because I did not want to go to Africa. So I dated Sigurd for about 3 years.

The hotel Solskin where Vera worked

The Hotel

It wasn't long before I got tired of working at the high school because I wasn't getting paid enough working there. So I got a job in Liseleje in a summer hotel serving food for all different kinds of people.

People came from all over the world that first year. In the evenings after work, my friend and I would go down to the beach to swim. At the beach we would see all these movie stars and all these beautiful people from all over the world laying in the sand, swimming in the water or walking along the beach. They had beautiful bathing suits and all kinds of nice clothing. I said to my friend that I worked with "Aren't they beautiful, those girls? Oh, aren't they nice!" And my friend said "Have you ever looked at yourself?" I said "What!?" She said "When you get home, take a good look at yourself and compare yourself with them. I think you will find that you are just as good looking yourself." I was kind of shocked because I had only ever thought of myself as a working girl, not a beauty. When I walked home later that day, there was a mirror in my room and I looked into it. Suddenly I realized "My goodness, I'm not bad looking myself." It is funny how you can see yourself one way but others can see you in a different way.

Right beside the hotel was what they called a "Kaserne", (barracks) with soldiers in it. They would usually come in to the hotel and eat and have a beer. I liked serving food because I got a lot of tips. It didn't matter to me if they were soldiers or not. I would treat everyone just the same. I was happy there.

3. THE START OF WW2

In the words of Vera as told to her son Willy

Time went by and summer came to an end so I went back home to help my dad with his mail for the winter. The next summer I was still not married and I went back to the summer hotel to work for another season. Everything was great and it was the same routine as the previous year. But when this summer was over, the war started.

After World War One it took some years before the economy started to get back on it's feet again. Things started to get a little better around the time I became a teenager. It seemed at that time, every time I was in a room with some grown ups all I ever heard them talk about was the fact that Hitler was rising down there in Germany and how everybody suspected that someday he would come to our country and give us all lots of trouble. They spoke of wars and destruction and it was very scary. I always worried when I heard them talk about it. So when the Second World War began my mind was already filled with frightening stories.

The Second World War started on the 3rd of September, 1939. The Germans were not yet in Denmark but I remember hearing on the hotel radio that the war had begun. It was the end of the season for the hotel and we were just getting ready to close up the hotel because the summer season ended in the first week of September. So myself and my friend from work went to the other end of Denmark, to Copenhagen on the ferry. On the boat I met a lot of people that I knew and everyone was talking about the war and they were all worried about it. I spent the winter again helping my dad with the mail.

It so happened that in April I had helped a man whose wife had died and had two young kids. I had said that I would help them out as a live in nanny until it was time for me to go back to the summer hotel. In the wee hours of the morning of April 9th ,1940, while I was there, I was sound asleep when I was awoken by a loud noise. I thought "That is funny, why is the threshing machine on that early in the morning? That's hard to understand. Why are they doing that?". The sound kept going on and on and on. So I went to my window, and what did I see? Airplanes. Airplanes. Millions of them. Millions! They flew right over the farm where I worked.

They flew so low I could read the numbers on them. And they kept coming and coming and coming. There were a couple of men standing there looking up. I remember them saying "Fantastic! Look at that! Oh boy!"

So I got dressed, ran down to the kitchen and turned the radio on, and what did I get? The Germans had taken over the radio station and they had a Danish person speaking for them. They said "We are the German army. We have come to Denmark to help you; to protect you from the English. But if you try to fight us in any way or form, we will fight you back by water, by land and by air. So you do what we tell you, and we will give you instructions. We will come on this radio station every half an hour and you listen, and you follow orders. This is the German army speaking to you." the very first instructions they gave us was that we had to darken our windows. No lights were to be seen. We had to be sure that no light shone out.

Later I heard from others how the Germans had come in the middle of the night. There were Danish soldiers that worked on the border between Denmark and Germany and the the Germans suddenly came and captured them, took them prisoner and killed some of them. That was the beginning of the Germans coming into our country.

I was just young and one of the first thoughts I had, believe it or not, was that it was a bit of a relief because now I didn't have to hear all of the stories from the grown ups about what will happen or what they will do; now I can see for myself day by day what they were going to do. Oh, and believe me, I saw it all right.

Back To The Hotel

So on May 1st, 1940, I went back to my beloved Liseleje and the summer hotel. By the hotel was the barracks where the soldiers lived. But now there were no Danish soldiers anymore. Now it was German soldiers living there. They would come into the hotel every day and now I had to serve food and beer to them instead. I could not speak German and they could not speak Danish but they would always order "Ofenkartoffeln" which sounded much like the Danish "bagte kartofler" (baked potatoes). The language barrier wasn't that bad, but it was a strain on us.

There was one Jew who used to come to the hotel a lot. He lived in Copenhagen and he would come to the hotel every summer. But this summer he couldn't come anymore. He had been captured and I heard later that he had been killed by the Germans. There were many things that happened like that which we did not agree with but we had no control over them.

The Electrician

At that time I was a young girl, and the Germans like young girls. And many young girls liked the Germans and would date the soldiers. I never dated any of the German soldiers. Some of them were good looking but I never gave in to the temptation.

One night the lights went out all of a sudden throughout the whole hotel. The whole hotel was plunged into darkness. One of the German soldiers stood up and said "I am an electrician. Can I see your electrical panel." The woman who owned the hotel spoke German and she took the soldier up to where the electrical panel was. The soldier fixed the problem for us. The owner told me to give the soldier free coffee and dinner as thanks and so I did. The owner sat and talked with him for awhile and the soldier seemed like a nice man.

The next day I rode my bicycle to the store. On the way back I suddenly saw him there. I stopped for a minute to talk to him. The man who lived across the road yelled at me "How would you like to get your hair cut off? " That really scared me. That's what they did to girls so I took off home quick. That was about the closest I ever got to getting to know one of the German soldiers. I had my own boyfriend, Sigurd. So I thought anyway.

Making A Date

One afternoon there was a girl who was sitting, talking to a German soldier and he asked her to go on a date. She agreed. And he said "Could you come meet me at "neun" (nine)? " Her eyes widened . "Oh no!" she said. He looked sort of bewildered but thought that maybe nine was too late for her so he said " what about "halb neun" (8:30 or "half before nine")? Then she got very upset and ran away. What the soldier didn't know was that the German word "neun" sounded like the Danish word "nøgen" which means "naked". So the girl thought the soldier had asked her to come naked and when she didn't agree to that, then perhaps she could meet him half naked.

4. MAILMAN'S DAUGHTER

Vera getting the mail

In the words of Vera as told to her son Willy

The first summer of the Second World War was now over and winter was approaching. I made my way home to help my father with the mail again. He was getting older and he wanted to work until he could get his full pension. By this point he was pretty close to having been carrying the mail for 40 years. I liked to help him and I didn't need any money for it because I made enough working at the summer hotel.

Winters were very cold and very hard in those days. I had to get up at five o'clock in the morning. My father would go to the post office and he would bring all the cards and letters and things home. We sat in the kitchen sorting it all out. There were 125 homes we had to deliver to over 32 kilometers. We broke the route into two. I would get half and he would get half. After we finished sorting the mail it would still be dark outside. We had to walk through the snow with heavy burdens and heavy papers. We had to carry the mail into people's houses. They had no mailboxes; they just left the doors unlocked so we could walk in. It was bitterly cold out. My mitts would get very, very wet.

While we were out delivering mail, everyone else in the area were all in bed sleeping because they couldn't afford to use the hydro to light their houses that early in the morning because of the war. The houses were dark and no one was awake except for people's dogs. I really liked dogs so I got talking to a lot of dogs. I had a small flashlight which I used to make sure the right mail was delivered to the right people.

After I walked for an hour or so I saw a light would come on way, way off in the distance. It happened every morning. When I saw that light it cheered me up and I thought to myself "I will soon be there, I will soon be there". I knew who it was. It was a house where a bricklayer lived and he had a house keeper. When I got there, every morning for the whole winter, the house keeper would answer the door and she would look and say "Ohh! The mailman's little girl! Come on in and have some coffee. " And she would take my wet mitts off, and my hat off, and my scarf and put them in the oven to dry. She would have coffee and buns ready for me. That happened every morning and I never forgot it. She was a very nice person. After I had my coffee and buns and my mitts were dry, I felt like a new person and I felt like I could walk forever from place to place.

When I came home my mom was still in bed because my dad had told her "You have to stay in bed as much as possible because we don't have any fuel to heat the house". We lived on an island and the transportation were absolutely nil. The Germans had taken all the transportation so we couldn't get anything across the fjord, so we had to use very very little. Hydro was very, very scarce also.

So when I came home from my route, I would wake up my mom and she would get up. We had a tiny little stove that we would light up just long enough to cook our meals. On the little stove we would heat some hot water to put in a hot water bottle to put under the blankets. We would not stay up for very long. I would go upstairs and go to bed. I remember waking up and under the blankets there would be ice on the blankets where I had been breathing; from my breath. That happened every morning, all winter. It was so very, very cold that winter.

Good Bye Sigurd
One day in the winter there was a letter for me. It was from

Sigurd's sister. I opened it up and read it and it said "Your boyfriend, Sigurd, has left. He went to Germany to help the Germans. He has turned Nazi. He likes Hitler and is very impressed by the German military. Sigurd had liked the military and now there was none in Denmark, because the Germans had taken care of that. He thought the Germans were fantastic and he was impressed and now he wanted to be with them. My mom is so upset that she could not sleep for 4 nights. She told me to write to you, to tell you." After I read the letter I put it in the stove and I burnt it up. I never saw Sigurd again, and I couldn't care less. He was a traitor, and I didn't care about him any more. And that was the end of him.

Ejvind (Ivan) Jorgensen

Hello Ivan
When winter was over I did not go back to the summer hotel like I had in the years past. I took a job in Copenhagen, in a different hotel. It was very nice and I worked there for awhile.

While I was working at the hotel, a high school reunion was organized for the school where I had taken my high school courses. I decided to attend since there was a train going right by the hotel that I could take. There was still war and the war seemed to be getting worse. But I went to the student reunion because I felt like seeing people that I used to know. When I got there, I met Ivan who was also at the student reunion.

Ivan and his dog Rossi (7th from the right) – Police dog training

During the years that I had not seen him, he had become a policeman and worked training police dogs. He had given up on becoming a missionary in Africa because it was impossible to travel during the war. When he saw me, he invited me out for a cup of coffee in a nearby little restaurant and we went there by ourselves. It was just the two of us and we had a nice time together. We became very good friends with each other again.

It didn't take too long before he gave me a ring and we were engaged. We started to set a date for the wedding. He wanted to get married right away. He had a job and he thought it was time. I said that "I don't really think that we should because there is no food and nothing we can buy. I don't know if I can keep house with all these rations." And he said "Oh I will help you, I will help you. I think that we should get married." So we set the date for 2nd of August, 1941. Now we had other things to think about besides

27

the war because we were getting ready for a wedding. So we both told our families about the decision. I wrote to my mom and she said "That is fine. Come home and help me get ready for the wedding". So I quit my job and I went home to Mors again. My mom and I got busy planning a wedding.

Vera and Ivan - married August 2nd, 1941

Carsten

So now suddenly I was a married woman. Ivan and I moved into an apartment in Valby. We were in Apartment 18 on the bottom floor of a great big building. Ivan was working in a police station in Copenhagen which was a long way from where we lived. But it was almost impossible to find places to live so we had to take what we could get. We had to bicycle to get through the city. But we were married and we were happy and pretty soon I knew that I was pregnant. I was very happy about that but I was also unsure though because you couldn't buy kids clothes, you couldn't buy blankets and you couldn't buy diapers. Everything was hard to get. So I went from store to store for the next few months trying to collect things for the coming baby. I never did get everything I needed, so I had to get some wool from my mom and some material left over from the neighbours to make things. So time went by and on April 17th, 1942 my first baby arrived. It was a boy and we called him Carsten.

After I had Carsten, of course I had more to do. I would take him in his baby carriage and walk him around and talk to him. When Carsten was about two months old, Ivan and I took Carsten for a little stroll down the street. We were right on the corner when we suddenly heard a huge explosion. We did not know what it was or where it came from. We just stood on the corner and soon we heard the sound of an ambulance. We couldn't get across the street because the ambulance was coming fast. As we stood at the same corner we counted 13 ambulances going by with their sirens on. We never did find out where the explosion came from or where the ambulances went because the Germans had control over the newspapers and radios and they never told people what was going on.

5. LIVING THROUGH THE WAR

In the words of Vera as told to her son Willy

I will tell you about a few incidents that happened during the war. Of course there were many, but here are just a few of them.

The Glass Door

One day the Germans decided to take over a bus station. They came by right where we lived. It happened to be a day when people were off work. The people did not like the Germans taking the bus station. Demonstrators came out into the streets yelling and screaming in protest. I was sitting in my window looking across at the young people yelling and screaming and I could see the German trucks going one way and the other. In the back of the trucks were the German soldiers. One of the trucks stopped and let out one soldier and then continued on to where the bus station was. The one soldier who had gotten out was now behind all the yelling people on the street and he knelt down with his machine gun pointing at all those people. Without thinking, I opened my window and yelled out "Watch Out!" The people started to disperse and so then the German pointed his gun at me. We had a glass door on the building next to my window and he shot down the glass door with his machine gun. Of course I had ducked down and luckily he did not get me.

Lili Marlene

A popular song that was played in those days was "Lili Marlene" and it was sung all over Denmark; all over Europe, actually. Ivan was a police man, and in his patrol area there was something called "Nyhavn". In it was a canal going almost right into the city. It was a harbour for sea going ships and boats. Ivan was on patrol there at night. He heard the Danish sailors had changed that song to propaganda against Hitler and they were singing it. He came home and told me how it sounded now. He was actually laughing at it. The Germans did not understand it because it was in Danish.

I det Tyske Rige er der luftalarm.
Ude paa gaden haster en kvinde med sit barn.
Hindes mand faar hun aldrig mere at se.
Han fandt sin dod i Rusland's sne.

Min gode Hitler mand,
du vil miste dine mænd.
Naar fra det kolde Rusland. Hitler vender hjem,
Saa er en rød lanterne det tegne han viser frem.
Men når han saa kommer til Berlin
Saa ligger alt ting i ruin.

Min gode Hitler mand, du mister snart dit land.
Kampen over Tyskland, byerne set i brand.
Snart vil vi overvinde denne grim mand.
Saa haenger vi Hitler i en strop
Ved siden af Von Ribbentrop
Min gode lille Hitler mand, du mister snart dit land."

Of course this is all in Danish. I will try to translate this to English.
It means:

"Down in Germany country there is an air raid.
Rushing into the bomb shelter, there is a woman with a baby.
Her husband she will never see again because he was found dead in the
Russian snow.
My good Hitler man you will lose your men.

From the cold, cold Russia, Hitler's coming back .
And now it's a red beacon the sign he has shown us.
When he comes into Berlin everything is in ruins
My good Hitler man, you will lose your land.

Battle over Germany. Cities are in flames.
Soon we will overcome this nasty man.

Then we will hang Hitler from a noose beside Von Ribbentrop
My good Hitler man, you will miss your men. "

It took the Germans a long time before they found out what those sailors were singing. But when they finally did, it was forbidden. The whole country was not allowed to sing or hum the tune of Lili Marlene.

Twenty Pounds Of Rice

There was a little grocery store in Copenhagen. They very, very, very, very seldom had stock on special things like rice, certain fruit and other things we just couldn't buy. But one time a ship came in and they had 20 pounds of rice that they sold to this little grocery store. The grocery man was weighing them out in ½ pound bags to sell them to his customers that came in there all the time.

So when he had started to sell them, suddenly a German soldier came out. He was alone; all by himself, walked up to the counter and said "I would like 20 pounds of rice". The grocery man had hidden the big bag and said "I am very sorry but I do not have 20 pounds of rice". The soldier said "Ok" and left.

Five minutes later the same soldier came back in, still with no weapons. He was unarmed but on each side of him was another soldier. Each of the other soldiers had a machine gun, and a helmet, and everything they needed to be forceful. The unarmed soldier went up to the grocer and said "I would like 20 pounds of rice." And guess what; now the grocer had rice.. And the soldier walked out the door with all the rice.

And that's the way the Germans operated in Denmark. The soldier could say that he was in there "unarmed". He could just ask for it and he got it.

Street Car

A German soldier stood under the alarm of a street car. But the street car had just begun to move. So he ran and tried to get in. Two Danish men put their hands out and helped the soldier into the street car. And the German soldier said "Danke schön" (which means 'thank you' in German).

The Danish men didn't understand and they said to each

other "Oh...he is going to Dam Holme! That's the other way!" So they took a hold of the German soldier and put him back out of the stop. And the German soldier was wondering "Hey! What in the world? First they helped me up and then they put me back out again!" Dam Holme was a street car stop but it was in the other direction.

6. GERMANS TAKE THE POLICE

Vera , Ivan and Carsten

In the words of Vera as told to her son Willy

In September 1944 Mrs. Larsen was living in Copenhagen for the winter. She had just come home from her hotel. She had phoned me and asked if I could come and help her one day because she wanted to have a party. I said I could because that week Ivan was sleeping in the daytime and at night he was at work.

So the day came when I was to go in to help her. Ivan came home from his police work, he had breakfast, and he went to bed. Carsten was 2 years old. We were going to take a street car to Mrs. Larsen's house. I went in to say good-bye to Ivan. We had our coats on and were going to go out the door when Carsten cried "I want to say good bye to my father! I want to say good bye to daddy!" And I said "Well we are in a hurry; you can say that when we come back." And then we left. We got into the street car and we were on our way.

When we were about half way to where Mrs. Larsen lived suddenly the street car stopped. And people in the street car got very upset because most of them were going to work and they had to be at work at a certain time. So they started yelling "Why don't we keep going?", "What is wrong?", "We want to be to work on time!", "What is stopping us?" And the conductor said "I don't know, but I advise anybody in a hurry to get out and walk because it could be all day." So most people got out of the street car, including me.

I took Carsten in my arms and started walking along the track of the street cars towards where I was going. As I walked there I counted the street cars. I remember I counted 40 of them, and they were all stopped of course. When I got to number 40 I found out what was stopping us. It was a German army truck. It was parked across the track. It was full of armed soldiers. They all had machine guns and helmets and the works. And they did not want to move. The Danish people were coming around and they were yelling and screaming and calling "Call the police! Call the police!" but no police came. Then someone said "Here come the German police." And then I started walking on because usually there is trouble when they show up.

So I walked on and on and of course I came late to Mrs. Larsen's place. It was about 10 a.m. when we got there and I explained to her why we were late. We were busy because we were running late and we got talking about what we needed to get done. She wanted to straighten up the rooms before noon and then do some baking in the afternoon. At about 11 a.m., just when we decided where to start the work, there was an air raid. So we talked about should we go to the shelter or should we ignore it? We decided to ignore it and start working.

Mrs. Larsen went into the bedroom beside the kitchen to clean. I was in the kitchen at about 12:30 when the phone rang. I went to the phone and it was Ivan. I was very surprised . I said "Ivan, what are you doing up? You are supposed to be sleeping." Ivan said "have you heard?" I said "No. What happened?" He said "I can not tell you over the phone. Stay there. I will come and get you. Do not go outside." So he hung up and just them Mrs. Larsen came out from where she was and said "I know what's happening. I heard two men talking outside. My window was open. I could hear them and they said the Germans are taking the Danish police." Just then we looked out the window and we saw four big German army trucks go by and in the back were full of Danish police and some German guards to watch them. They were on their way to concentration camps in Germany.

Mr. Larsen was working as a chef on a Greenland ship. His ship was laying in the harbour that day so he just came home. He told us that while he was at the ship he saw the Germans enter the sea police (the sea police are Danish coast guards), grab all the sea policemen, put them in a German truck and drove them away. It all happened at 11 o'clock just when the air raid alarm sounded. It was a phony alarm just to get all the policemen. Whenever an alarm went off the policemen all had to report for duty so the Germans used that to get them. There was no air raid or enemy planes at all. It was a trick. That was a bit shocking to hear.

Soon Ivan came and he told us that when he was asleep there was an air raid. The laws for the police at that time was that 6 hours after they were through their duty and had gone home, if there was an air raid they had to go back to work again. So he got up, put his uniform on, and bicycled towards work at the police station. Then people in the street yelled at him and shouted "Do not go to the police station! The Germans are shooting out of there and catching policemen! Don't go there!" So Ivan turned around, went home, took his uniform off, put his civil clothes on and phoned the station. A German answered. He wanted to know who Ivan was, where he was, and his telephone number. So Ivan hung up without answering. Then he called a baker who lived across from the Store Kongensgade police station which was where he worked. The baker said "It's going really bad, really bad. But I can't say anymore. But it's really bad." So Ivan hung up and that was when he phoned me.

But now he was here and he insisted that he wanted to go down to his station to see how things are. His police station is quite close to where we were. I didn't want him to go but he left anyway. But when he got there, there were no policemen what so ever. But there were German guards all around the building. There was absolutely nothing he could do so he came back up to where

Carsten and I were. He said "We have got to leave immediately. So get ready." And we did.

We went downstairs. There is a porch in the building and we stood in the porch. Ivan had his bicycle with him and we put Carsten on it and Ivan and I would run along side it. But on the street we were supposed to follow they were shooting on both sides and the bullets where whining. It was all around us. It was very scary. We didn't know whether to go out or not go out. But then we heard a street car. We heard the bell ringing on the street car. We knew it would be the last one perhaps for days. And Ivan said "We've got to go! Now!" So we ran. We ran full speed through the shooting, through the street and to the street car. As we got there, the street cars were starting to move again. I grabbed Carsten off of the bicycle where he sat and went to the street car door while Ivan got on his bike and rode away. Two men helped me; got us up there while the street car was still moving. I got in, sat down and started to cry. I really had a cry. Nobody looked at me. Everybody knew. That was the only time I ever broke down and cried during the 6 years of war. But part of that might have been because I was 3 months pregnant with Willy at the time.

When I got home Ivan was already there and all the neighbours were all flocked around him. They all wanted to help him with something. One gave him a repair kit for his tires in case he had a flat tire on his bicycle. One gave him a piece of rope to tie a parcel on with. One man, Mr. Kristiansen, came and said "I will hold the key to your apartment for you and I will look after it for you until you come back." They were all so helpful. I went into the apartment and grabbed the necessary things, but only the very necessary. I got the toothbrushes, pajamas, maybe some underwear, but not very much. And we were off on our bikes.

The street that leads out is 15 kilometers long. We had 15 kilometers on bicycles to get out of the city. On the way we thought "What if there are guards on the border and they see us and want to see our I.D.?" On Ivan's I.D. it says "policeman". We would never get out. We were worried about that. We met another bicycle man. He was a policeman too and he was worried about the same thing. But when we got to the border there were no guards there. They were too busy in the city. And that was very lucky for us.

After we got through the city border we started talking about where we should go. Ivan said he had an uncle, Valdemar Pedersen, who lived about 50 kilometers away. We would try to go there and see if we could sleep there tonight. So we did. Ivan didn't show that he was tired but he hadn't slept all night. With all the confusion and things he must have been very tired.

When we finally got there to his uncle's in Hvalsø (that was the name of the town) they greeted us with open arms. Valdemar's son, Jens, who was also a police officer, and his wife and six month old baby girl were also there hiding out. "Come in! Come in! We're so happy! We heard about the police being taken over by the Germans and we were worried about you. Come in and you can stay here!" That was a help. So we seemed to be ok there for awhile.

Nobody knew where we were but we were still wondering about what was going to happen to us and what we were going to do with ourselves.

Cleaning The Apartment

Meanwhile I went in, off and on, to our old apartment to bring out a few things that we needed; like clothes and things. Also there were things in there that should be removed because Mr. Kristiansen, who had the key, told me something happened that he didn't like.

One evening a bunch of Germans had come in. They were Gestapo, not soldiers, and they came in with flashlights and they shone their light on all the names of who lived in the apartment building. They tried to get in the door where we used to be but of course it was locked. They didn't find anything that on the outside of the door to indicate that a policeman lived there so they left. But should they come back and go into the apartment then that would be a different story.

When he saw them there he got a little worried about looking after our apartment. So he asked me if he could go with me in there and if we could remove things that showed that a policeman lived there. We were lucky to have the Kristiansens to look after our place. We had heard that some of the other policemen had tried to move their furniture. The Gestapo had followed them and found out where they had moved to and arrested them.

So Mr. Kristiansen, his wife, and myself went in together. There were several things that had to be removed. We removed his uniform, some papers, police magazines, some addresses, etc. When I thought I was finished Mrs. Kristiansen pointed at the daily calendar that still showed the date Tuesday September 19th, the day they took the police in September. Also there was a gun. The gun I had hidden downstairs in the store room. So I did not take it out the same day as the other things. It was very, very risky to go around with a police gun. So we left the gun down there. Everything else we had removed. And I went to different places to straighten out our business and things because we intended to move so that they wouldn't find us.

A few days later I came back again. I did that for Ivan. I got other things removed and I went to the bank. I remember because we had gotten word secretly from some other police organization that Ivan could get paid. So I went to the bank and picked that up for him.

Ivan (on the right) doing some gardening

New I.D.
Ivan couldn't do much. He couldn't move because all his papers said "policeman" on them. And as soon as he went out the Germans would find out he is a policeman and they would grab him. So we had to do something about that.

We had a friend, Hans Olsen, who worked in Copenhagen in City Hall and we got in touch with him somehow. He promised to make a new I.D. card for Ivan so that he could travel on the train without getting caught. And he did so. This one said "Ivan Jorgensen – Gardener". I took the train, went in there, and got his new card. But I was worried about how to bring it back because I would be checked. On the train or the bus or however I was traveling, I would be checked by the Germans and if I was caught with a brand new I.D. card with somebody else's name on it they would be wondering what I was up to. But I had Carsten with me. He was only two. He had a pocket in his suit; a breast pocket. Somehow I got that card into his pocket without him seeing it and buttoned it up. Children did not get inspected. So I got into the train with Carsten who had the new I.D. in his pocket and we brought it safely home to Ivan. He was very happy. Now he could go on trains, go on the ferry, and travel around without showing the Germans that he really was a policeman.

The Gun

Now since Ivan had gotten his I.D. corrected and he was more free to travel, it made him feel a lot better. He had a friend in Odense (you have to go there by ferry) who offered him a job as a gardener. And that was great because that was where Ivan's parents were. So he went over there by himself and left me and Carsten with his uncle. After he got over there I got a letter from him. It said that he would very much like to have his police gun and could I get it to him one way or another because he needed it. He had joined a secret organization against the Germans that the police force had made up. But he needed his gun.

It was very risky to go around with a gun because it was very much against the German's law to have a gun or to carry a gun. Anybody who had a firearm, weapon or gun or anything like that was supposed to deliver it to the German headquarters. But Ivan wanted his gun. So one day I went into the Kristiansen's again. I did not take Carsten this time because my mission was to get that gun and get it over to Ivan. When I got there I went up to Kristiansens and I told them about it. And they were going to help me. I had a little mattress for my baby carriage. I intended to sew the gun and the ammunition into the mattress and mail it to Ivan. I talked to Mrs. Kristiansen and she understood and everything was good.

So I went down in the store room in the basement. I got the gun, I wrapped it in newspaper and I carried up to the Kristiansens on the third floor. But when I got there, they had a visitor. A lady was sitting there talking to them. I was a bit scared about that because anyone who wanted to give me up would get $100 to report me and the gun. You just couldn't trust anyone these days. So I put the gun wrapped in newspaper down in the corner of the kitchen with a remark "Here is the stuff I brought for you". I don't think the lady knew what it was. It seemed forever that she sat and sat and sat, but finally she left.

I went down to my apartment and got the mattress. Then Mrs. Kristiansen and I locked the door and got busy. We sewed the gun into the middle of the mattress and the ammunition all around. We wrapped it in paper, put the address on it, and tied the string around it. I took the parcel and walked down the sidewalk towards the post office.

When I got almost to the post office, on the street were a whole bunch of German soldiers marching and singing the German song. And just when they were right beside where I walked, they all came up on the sidewalk. I literally had to push my way through them. I was so scared, I could hear my own heart hammering inside me. I've never been so scared. The day before I had seen the Germans stop a man on the sidewalk and make him open his parcel. So I thought they may do that to me, but they didn't and I took it to the post office. I was very, very relieved when the post office took my parcel.

The Girls In The Bakery

I was very happy when I got a letter from Ivan saying that he had received the gun without any problems. So now I am free to travel over there to be with him. He was living with his parents in Odense. I got ready, packed up, left his uncle and arrived in Odense.

We lived with Ivan's parents. They were very good to me. By now I was 5 months pregnant with Willy. So when we went there we had a bedroom in his parents house and Ivan was working as a gardener. In the beginning it seemed to be going fairly well.

Then one day a man came and knocked on the door. Ivan's grandmother went to the door and this strange man said "Well, I thought I should tell you, I was just in the bakery and I heard two girls who work there talking about your house and your people. And they said 'It's a wonder, we see a new person going up and down the stairs all the time. He's a tall man, and he came here recently. We are pretty sure it's one of these stray policemen. And if we tell the German soldiers we would get one hundred dollars. That would be an easy way to make money'."

By this time Ivan's mother had also come to the see who was at the door and had been listening to him. This strange man said to my mother-in-law "I just thought I would tell you." And she said "Thank you" because these girls were right.

So now Ivan had to be more careful living with his parents. And he had to move away. He didn't always stay there over night. He had three brothers in the town. So he took turns sleeping here and there. Sometimes he slept where I was, but not all the time.

The Man On The Road

In Odense, while I was there with my mother-in-law one morning, we were just out of bed and we had breakfast and then we were going to do house work. My mother-in-law was watering her flowers in the big window towards the street. I was playing with Carsten on the floor. Suddenly my mother-in-law said "It's a strange thing. Right at my neighbours there across the street in the bungalow. There are four men with machine guns walking around on their roof."

So I go over and look and sure enough there are four men walking on the roof with machine guns. And on the ground in the driveway was a telephone truck. So we stood and watched them. Suddenly they started shooting and we thought, well we had better move away from the window. So we moved back a bit but we still kept an eye on them.

After awhile we saw one man, but that was a different man. He had a long German overcoat on and he came out from that driveway. He was hanging on to everything he saw. He was hanging onto the fence, and then to the buildings. And suddenly he collapsed on the road. There was a stream of blood coming from behind him and where he lay.

A whole lot of people, I think there were 200 people, were standing around him, looking, looking, talking. But nobody touched him. I thought it was very funny; very strange. We couldn't understand it. But the ones on the roof had disappeared. There was some shooting though, before it happened. We heard some shooting.

And we stood and looked. Suddenly I see my husband down there, Ivan. He was one of the spectators. He was down there looking at this man who appeared to be dead.

Suddenly an ambulance came. They picked up the man and disappeared. Then Ivan came up where we were. I remember meeting him in the doorway and saying "Oh Ivan! Why didn't you help the poor guy? He was laying there so helpless with blood streaming out from him." Ivan said "Why should I help him? He was a German Gestapo."

After that my mother-in-law was a bit curious because she knew the people in the bungalow. So she went over there. She talked to the woman. And the woman said "Well, I must admit, my husband is in the underground soldiers. And these 4 Germans came. They had come in and I was doing my washing. I have a baby; a six month old. They came in and demanded to find out where my husband was. But he wasn't there. He was not home. So they sat down, without asking, at my kitchen table and sat and talked German to each other. They wouldn't move. Every so often they used the phone to phone their headquarters to find out if they still had to wait there. I suppose that is what they phoned for. But they kept sitting there for a long, long, long time.

Well it seems to appear that while they were still sitting there, the 4 Danish underground soldiers came in the telephone truck because apparently they had tapped the phone so they knew the Germans were there. They didn't come in. They stayed outside on the roof waiting for the Germans to come out. After awhile when the Germans finally came out they shot them all. Three of them died in my yard. The fourth one laid outside and he died too." That was the one I saw.

When these Germans first came in, this lady was outside hanging the washing. She threw her 6 month old baby over the fence to the neighbours hoping the neighbours would take care of the baby. And the neighbours did. They saw the baby, took it in and took care of it. So now everything was ok in their family as far as that goes.

7. PEACE IS FLEETING

Vera and Carsten with Ivan's parents, Laurits and Johanna

In the words of Vera as told to her son Willy

So I lived on, with my in-laws, in Odense and I got more and more pregnant of course. My baby was getting bigger. I needed a maternity dress and couldn't get any. There were no new dresses anywhere. I went into a second hand dress shop and they said they would get me one but I had to wait. There were 100 ahead of me. So I knew that was hopeless. I would have that baby before I would ever get the dress. So I gave that up.

My mother-in-law had a little piece of cloth. She added on to my ordinary dress. She made a hole in the front and sewed the piece of cloth in. My coat couldn't be buttoned so I had to go with it open. It was winter at that time. But anyways, we managed.

On the 25th of March, it was a Sunday, I woke up and knew it was the day. So all the men of the house disappeared, except Ivan. My father-in-law and Ivan's brothers suddenly disappeared. They took Carsten with them. The mid-wife came and before we knew it, we had a baby boy. And we named him Willy.

Willy age 18 months

Willy's First Day Out

When Willy was 3 weeks old, it was on a Sunday morning, I borrowed Gordon and Ludia's baby carriage (Gordon was Ivan's brother) and decided to take him for a ride outside for the first time. So I had Willy in the carriage and Carsten walking beside me. We got out in the street in Odense. It was such a beautiful, beautiful April morning. The birds were singing and everything seemed so peaceful. The weather was beautiful and I was happy to be getting out. Carsten was walking beside the baby carriage and we were walking slowly up the street. We kept walking and because it was so nice out I almost forgot about the war.

My father-in-law had a garden at the other end of the city. It was called a "colony garden". This was a garden we loved to go to. There was a bench and some flowers and a little hut. So we ended up there. As we got there I could see a lot of other people there working in the garden, planting flowers and doing things. It was so beautiful. I sat on the bench .

Suddenly we had an air raid. And just then, everybody in the gardens around me just jumped on their bicycles and disappeared. I found myself completely alone with the two kids. And I knew it was not a safe place to be.

So I hurried up and put Carsten into the baby carriage and ran. I tried to find a shelter somewhere. I ran down the street of

Odense. The street was completely empty. There was nobody but me. Everybody had gone to shelter. And the air raid was noisy.

Suddenly I saw a man on a bicycle coming from the other side of the road. He stopped in front of a house. He waved at me and yelled "Come over here!" I ran across the street over to him. I said "Do you live here?" He said "No. But we need shelter."
So he went to the door . The door was unlocked but there was nobody in the house. He helped me to carry the carriage inside the house. Then he looked around. He found a shelter in the basement that had sand bags for the windows. He came up and helped me to carry the carriage down to the basement where we were safe we thought.

So we sat there. We could hear the noises outside. We could hear all the confusion. There were ambulances driving, there was whining, there was bombing. Everything was awful. I think we sat there an hour, at least. Then finally we got the siren meaning "You can come out now. Everything is all right".

So he helped me to carry the carriage upstairs. And we got out to the street. I never saw the man before or after. I don't know his name, but he sure helped me that day.

And I started towards my in-laws house. Long before I got to the house I saw them, the whole family, outside. It was my father-in-law, my mother-in-law, Ivan, and his brother Gordon. They all stood there with their hand up over their forehead, staring down, here and there on the road trying to have a look. They were looking for me. They had no idea where I was. And when I came they were very, very happy to see me. They never even got mad at me for wandering so far away.

Happy Peace

And then time went on for a little while and we came to May the 5th, 1945. And that was the official day of peace; when the Germans had given up the fight.

And in the morning early, when we woke up, it came over the radio and everybody was so happy. Everybody came out in their pajamas and their nightgowns wishing each other "Happy Peace!" It didn't matter where you went, people were yelling "Happy Peace! Happy Peace!" Everybody was happy. After six long years of war we were finally free! And that was all you heard on the radio, on the street, in the house; everybody. "Peace!" they say,

"Peace!" they say.

Carsten's and Willy's grandfather gave them each a little flag. I got the baby carriage again. They had flags with them and everybody went down the street to celebrate. The streets were full of people. Everybody, whether they knew each other or not, were shaking hands and were yelling "Happy Peace!" It was just so wonderful.

At night we were finally able to take the darkened blankets down from the windows. Everyone in all the houses had candles glowing in the windows in celebration.

Vera

The Letters

A Letter from Vera to her mother Sine

Odense May 5th, 1945

Dear Mom and Dad,

Hard to believe we are free again. Today everybody in this city are decorated with Danish flags and their spirits are very high. Finally, after 6 years of war we are a free country. This morning the radio is free, all the church bells are ringing, and everyone is really excited. I was out of bed and down in the yard at 7 o'clock this morning. Carsten and Willy were still sleeping. The neighbours came out in their night gowns and p.j.'s and wished each other "Happy Peace" and "Good Luck".

I went into the house, washed and dressed Carsten and Willy. Ivan's dad gave them each a Danish flag. I took the boys for a walk down the street; Willy in Allan's baby carriage and Carsten walking beside us. As we were leaving, Gordon and Lydia came from the country. They wanted to celebrate in the city.

The first thing we saw on the street was a parked truck. Two guerilla soldiers with machine guns and helmets had stopped the traffic. They were out to catch stikkers*. We stayed awhile and watched the guerillas bring out several persons. They seemed to know where to find them. There were six guerillas all together. The streets were soon crowded with people. They booed and yelled "Shoot them on the spot!" We walked on to the police station where they brought the stikkers. Then I went home to Ivan's dad's to feed Willy. He is about 6 weeks old now. He is growing fast.

In the afternoon we all went down town again; the whole family, and everybody's families. The streets were so full of people. Suddenly shooting started on the streets. We were almost home by that point and we hurried into the house. The shooting got worse.

Richard and Doris and their son Bjørn, who were up near the police station, had to take shelter under a parked truck for about an hour. The shooting lasted about 3 to 4 hours. Fourteen people were killed and many more were wounded. I don't know who they were. I know one was a policeman. Glad I got home safe with Willy and Carsten. I heard people say that it was the Germans and German helpers trying to free or help the arrested stikkers from this morning.

Ivan went back to Copenhagen last Thursday. He wanted to be there at the police station when he was needed. It is hard to believe that just last week he was still underground, but now he can come out in the open. Hope he will be O.K. I'm sure there will be trouble there too. It will be awhile before things settle down and get back to normal. I would have liked to have gone with him, but it is so unsafe to travel. Should be better soon.

Really nice that we can write and talk free again.

Love Vera

* Stikkers is a word meaning a Danish person who had sided with the Gestapo during the war and sold out their own men and country for money

Odense May 8th, 1945

Dear Mom and Dad,

Today I took Carsten and Willy in Allan's baby carriage to down town Odense. The English soldiers have now moved into the city here. There were thousands of them. They were driving army trucks and jeeps very slowly. They drove through the streets like a parade. They were shaking people's hands. Carsten and I spent all day shaking dirty soldiers hands. The people were excited. They shook hands and shouted "Hoorah! Hoorah!" We did too.

When we came home to Carsten's Farfar and Farmor, Carsten ran around shook hands with everyone there, and said "You are supposed to yell 'Hoorah! Hoorah!' to me." He was playing English soldier.

Ivan is okay. He is back in the police force again in Copenhagen. I would like to go back too. Traveling is very crammed right now. Lots of sea mines in Store belt too. We will wait a few days. The mine destroyers are out there.

Today the Germans are marching out of the city here. They look somehow very tired, but, there are lots of them. They are walking now.

I will soon go back to Copenhagen again and get back to normal after 6 years. Willy weighs almost 11 pounds now.

Love from Carsten, Willy and Vera

A Letter from Vera to her mother Sine

Copenhagen May 30th, 1945

Dear Mom and Dad,

Nice to be home again. Everything is O.K. Here. We had left in such a hurry. We were lucky to have the Kristiansens to look after our place. We heard later that when some of the other policemen tried to move their furniture, the Gestapo had followed them and found out where they had moved to. Then they knew where to find the policemen and they arrested them.

While we were still in Hvalsø, I went back to the apartment to get some clothes and things. Mr. Kristiansen, the man who held our keys and looked after our things, came to me and told me that one night a German Gestapo truck came to our apartment building . They went into the hallway and, with a flashlight, read the names on the doors. Mr. Kristiansen thought that they were looking for Ivan. He was very uneasy about it and said that he didn't want to be involved with the Gernmans. This time the Germans had left without breaking in because they didn't find anything on the outside door to indicate a policeman lived there. But, should they come back and come into the apartment it would be a different story. So we went in and removed all the evidence that a policeman lived there.

Everyday Germans came over the radio to tell the Danish people that it was unlawful to own or keep a gun of any kind. Anyone who had a gun was to bring it to the German headquarters. Of course we were not about to go to the Germans and say "Hello there, I just happen to have a gun". Besides Ivan wanted his gun. So I told the Kristainsen's that we had decided to mail the gun to Ivan by sewing it into a small baby crib mattress. They thought this was a good idea and offered to help with packaging it up. I think they were glad to get it out of the building as there was a big penalty for hiding a gun or to help hide a gun, or know anyone who had a gun.

I had to walk to the post office with it once it was packaged up. When I turned the first street corner, there were about 100 German soldiers marching straight towards me. Suddenly they all came up on the sidewalk and I literally had to push my way between them with my big parcel. I had never been so scared in my life. I was so afraid they would open my parcel for inspection. Well, they didn't and I was awfully glad to reach the post office and have them take it out of my hands. I was even more relieved when I got a letter from Ivan saying that he had received the parcel in good condition.

Willy weighs 13 pounds now. He is a happy baby and so easy to care for.

Love Vera

8. GOING TO CANADA

In the words of Vera as told to her son Willy

The ship "Georgic" they came to Canada on in May of 1951

And now since the war was over, Ivan traveled back to his police job in Store Kongensgade , Copenhagen. And very shortly after, the two kids and I went there too. And now things seem to be back to normal again.

After awhile, Ivan, who had been working for the gardener for awhile, got a little tired of police work in the big city. So he decided he wanted to buy a little piece of land. And he did out in Risby. And then he started making a little business for himself out there. First he did it together with his police work. Then he could take a year off and he could come back to the police if he wanted to or he could stop and do another business. He took a year off and worked up there and it seemed to go fine. So he quit his police job and worked as a gardener in his own garden.

But then we had problems because the country was run down. He couldn't buy a car to sell the stuff. We had to have somebody else to bring it to market. So therefore, it wasn't as good as we had hoped.

Meanwhile all the French started to go to Canada. It was quite common that people emigrated to Canada. Canada was a much better country than Denmark at the time. Ivan got the idea that we should go there. I didn't want to go. I said "Well if we wait we will have money from the crops coming up. Ivan said "Too slow"." I said "We have to wait. We have to have patience." He said "No, no, no. We gotta go." He kept on about it.

52

When it was Christmas we went over to his family again. And his brother was going over to Canada. That really did it. Now he was after me. "We should go to Canada". I argued "No, I don't want to go to Canada. I want to stay here".

Then he said "Do you know that the next thing that is going to happen here is the Russians are going to come and take over Denmark. They will take our kids and raise them up their way." And I was thinking about that and I said "Well okay. If you want to go to Canada then let's go."

Immediately we went for an application. It was already 1951 by now. We sold of what we had and in May of 1951 we were on the big ship on the way to Canada.

At Sea

A Composition from Vera to her English Teacher

We were only at sea for eight days and eight nights. But it seemed like an everlasting journey. The two thousand passengers aboard, crowded the ships deck like a swarm of insects. They were desperately trying to settle down and enjoy the thrill of the adventure, like a five year old on his first fishing trip. But, on the third day only half of those excited passengers came for lunch. The rest were in their cabins all crinkled up in their bunk beds, twisting and turning like snakes, trying to overcome the seasickness brought on by the restless sea.

They didn't have much luck, however, for the very next night we heard a howling whistling like the sound of a charging dragon. The passengers started to hoot and holler. There was a confusing mingling of sounds like the cries of wild beasts. But, as it seemed, it didn't impress the restless Atlantic ocean. She writhed with the storm like a whale in labour pain. It was a long sleepless night for the two thousand passengers. The ship creaked and shrieked and groaned like a ghost town during a hurricane.

Then suddenly things changed. The sea became calm and the ship just lulled like one would lull a baby to sleep. We all took advantage of the situation; we jumped into our bunk beds ready to be lulled to sleep.

Suddenly a powerful, hoarse toot- toot sound was heard. It was answered by a sickly sound from the distance. The sickly sound, however, came clearer and clearer and became louder and louder until it sounded like a charging elephant. The fog was heavy and the fog horns were in constant use. Their prolonged, harsh signals of warning were frightening. It was as if we were being attacked by "The Flying Dutchman".

We were all in the same boat. Half of us were still with turning stomachs; the rest of us were trying to see through the vaporized atmosphere hoping Canada would show up very soon.

I See Trees

In the words of Vera as told to her son Willy

After eight days in the ship (the ships name was Georgic. It was an English ship) we landed in Halifax. I remember it was supper time. We were sitting, eating when the waiter looked up and he said "I see trees". And everybody jumped up and looked out. And we were coming into Halifax. It was really nice. But we had to sleep on the ship all night.

The next morning we got out. We had to go through customs and all that stuff. We got on a train towards Toronto. But we actually had a job in Windsor. But they told us to get off in Toronto. When we got to Toronto and got off the train and went into the Immigration Office they told us we did not have a job in Windsor and that they were supposed to get us a job. So we sat all day there waiting for them to find us a job. It took a long time. But finally they said we have a job with a lady, Mrs. Helm, who lived in King City on a farm and we could get there by bus. And she will pick us up at the bus station.

So we did go to the bus and got to King City. And when we got there, there was a lady, Mrs. Helm, waiting for us. She had a station wagon and a nice farm. She had two children, Peter and Anne. Peter was two years older than Carsten. Anne was two years older than Peter. So they got along very well. We stayed there for almost a year.

Anne Helm

While we were on the farm our two boys really enjoyed it there. They liked Peter; they played with him a lot. Anne was a very pleasant girl. She ended up as a movie star. She was in quite a few movies; Elvis Presley movies. And she was a very beautiful girl too.

Peter also went on to become an actor in television shows. He was in shows like "The Longest Day" and "Wagon Train" in the episodes of "The Daniel Clay Story", "The Wagon Train Mutiny", and "The Tom O'Neal Story". Later on he also worked in film production.

So that part of our lives was okay. At that time when you came to Canada from another country you were only allowed to bring $100 with you. But eventually we bought our own farm and worked around there and tried to get something out of it which we eventually did. It is a struggle to come to a strange country without money though.

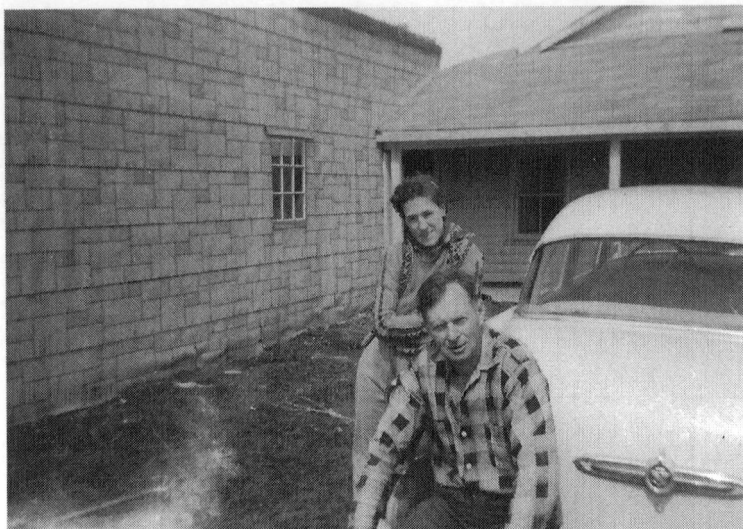

Vera and Ivan on their farm near Campbellford, Ontario, Canada

A Place Of Our Own

A narrative in the perspective of Willy written by Vera for her English Class

It was still quite dark in my room when I awoke. I could see a slim streak of light by the door indicating that the lights were on in the kitchen. I could also hear my father and mother talking to a stranger and it sounded like they were breaking down the stove pipes.

I rubbed my eyes and tried to see through the dark. It was impossible. I could hear my brother breathing in the bed beside me. He was obviously still sleeping. I wanted to know the time and since my brother was nine and able to tell time on the alarm clock, I started to call him.

It was a little while before he reacted, but suddenly I heard a thump on the floor and the light was turned on. Carsten never climbed out of bed; he always jumped in a very athletic manner. He said "Oh Willy, it's only five a.m. But today we are going to move to the farm, remember. They are already loading the trucks"

Then we both eagerly started to get dressed. This was the start of a very important and eventful day. November 8, 1953, the day we loaded all our belongings onto two trucks and moved to our own farm.

9. LEARNING THE LANGUAGE

A Letter by Vera to her English Teacher

March 20, 1977

Dear Teacher 1066,

It has been a long winter hasn't it? But, everything comes to an end, and so does this English course. I just thought I would write you a small letter, and tell a little about my lack of education of the English language.

When we arrived in Canada on May 27, 1951 I didn't know a single word of the language spoken in this country. Our language was Danish, and we were using the metric system. I had lots to learn. I was unable to attend a school as we were way out in the country. We had no car or money, and I didn't have a driver's license either. So I began to listen when people were talking. In the beginning, it was impossible for me to hear where one word stopped and another began. After a while, when I began to single out words, I learned to understand some of them. Others were confusing and sounded so much alike that it was impossible for me to hear the difference. They were words like floor, flower and flour. Also, letter, litter, ladder and lettuce gave me trouble. But most of all, I think I had trouble hearing the different sounds of the words dog, duck, dock, doc (doctor) and Doug (Douglas). I never did take an English lesson, just kept on listening and eventually started to speak it.

In 1973, my husband bought a typewriter. I looked at it and wished that I knew how to type. Then I took a typing course at night school. After that, I began to wish that I knew more English. One of my friends introduced me to the correspondence courses which I didn't know about. I wrote them and explained my situation. As a result, I enrolled in "Basic English" or "E160" in the fall of 1974.

Recently I spoke to an 18 year old, grade 13 student. I told him about this course. He said "Oh that's easy". I answered "Yes, if you already took the grades one, two, three, four, five, six, seven, eight and nine. Otherwise you will have to work at it."

Our youngest son, Willy, was six years of age when we came to this country. After about two years I heard him say to a friend "When we first came here, we didn't know it was so easy to speak

57

English" Sure everything is easy if you know how.

I must run along, my dog Rex wants out. Thank you for everything. Have a good summer.

Sincerely yours,
Vera Jorgensen

Response to Vera from her English Teacher

Thank you for the letter. Your writing of the English language is better maybe, than that 18 year old. Keep at it. Good Luck!

Confusion Of The Language

A Composition About Her Friends from Vera to her English Teacher

My friends Ted and Elsa Kristensen, had been in Canada for about 9 months when they received word that their best friends from Denmark were emigrating as well and that they would arrive at a certain date. It was then arranged that Rigmor and her husband Esper would be staying at the Kristensen's apartment in Scarborough for a week or so.

The reunion brought happiness to both couples. They were all truly delighted to be together again. They surely talked many hours away and it was way past midnight before they finally went to bed on that first evening.

About two o'clock a.m. Ted and Elsa awoke because there was a frantic knocking on their bedroom door. They could hear Esper scream with a piercing voice "Ted! Elsa! Wake up! Wake up!"

They rushed out to Esper to find out what was wrong. He was very nervous as he explained "My wife is in her third month of pregnancy and she is losing the baby!"

Neither Esper not Rigmor Pedersen had any knowledge of the English language. Elsa only knew what she had picked up by ear during her nine months stay in Scarborough. Ted knew a little more, for he was working every day and had to communicate with his co-workers. But Elsa was the one who rushed to the telephone, picked up the telephone book, looked in the yellow pages, and found a doctor's address and telephone number.

She dialed. A calm voice on the other end said "Hello". Elsa explained in her broken English "Lady losing baby, what we do?" The doctor asked "How old is Lady?" Elsa put the receiver down, rushed to Rigmor's bedroom and asked "Rigmor, how old are you?" Rigmor looked puzzled, but answered with a weak voice "I am 30 years old".

Elsa hastened back to the telephone, picked up the receiver again and shouted nervously "Doctor, doctor, lady is 30 ye'r oll." Elsa thought she heard the doctor mumble to himself "impossible" but then he asked "What breed is Lady?"

Elsa did not understand the word "breed" and she thought the doctor had asked her if Rigmor was still breathing. It made Elsa very nervous and she stuttered "Ya-ee lady she- she sti--- still breading." The doctor then asked in his usual calm voice "I mean, what kind of a dog are you talking about?"

The Elsa realized her mistake. It was not a doctor for human beings, but a veterinarian she was talking to. She thanked her lucky stars that the veterinarian was a kind and helpful man. He made sure that Rigmor was put in the hands of a good doctor in one of Scarborough's fine hospitals.

Rigmor was taken into emergency by a nurse. Another nurse appeared and wanted some papers filled out. And since Ted was the only one able to understand her, he and answered the questions. Then he also signed the papers.

An hour or two passed by before the nurse came back tot he waiting room. She signaled to Ted that he could now come and see Rigmor. All three of them protested. They tried to make the nurse understand that it was Esper, not Ted who was married to Rigmor. Esper was shoved away by two nurses saying "Not allowed, not allowed". He protested the best he could but in Danish. The nurses kept saying "Not allowed". Then they took Ted by the arm and led the way to Rigmor's bed. Ted tried his best to explain but finally gave up. He realized that he was the one who signed the admitting papers.

Willy and Carsten

Learning To Drive

In the words of Vera as told to her granddaughter Dana

I remember when we were first learning English, Willy and Carsten learned it faster because they were in school and Ivan and I were not. Eventually Ivan and I learned how to drive and got our driver's licenses. We would go together as a family on various outings. When we came to a road that had a red triangular Yield sign we asked Carsten and Willy what it said. They answered that it said "Yield". Not being able to distinguish between certain words, I thought they meant "Yell". So I thought that anytime you were going to merge with a Yield sign that you should yell to let people know you were coming. I thought this was very peculiar and wondered out loud why Canada would have such a strange law. When Willy and Carsten realized what I was thinking they had a good laugh and explained to me the difference between "Yield" and "Yell". But every time we came to a Yield sign, just for fun, we would stick our heads out the window and yell and shout "We are coming! Get out of the way! Here we come!"

10. FARM LIFE

In the words of Vera as told to her granddaughter Dana

Vera and Rex on the farm

Rex

Having a farm of our very own was a great feeling but it was also a lot of work. We had to get up very early in the morning, sometimes while it was still dark out, to get all of our chores done. The animals depended on us to do that.

We had many animals around the farm; cows, chickens, cats and dogs. I love dogs. Since I was not allowed to have another dog as a kid, I was very happy to be able to have our own dog on our own farm. We named this dog Rex. Rex was a German Shepherd . Since Ivan had trained police dogs when he was in Denmark, he trained Rex very well.

One day Mr. and Mrs. Jones, one of the neighbours, came to visit. Mrs. Jones was afraid of Rex so when he started barking at her she ran, screaming, from the door and back towards the car. Rex gave chase and caught up with her. Rex jumped up on her and grabbed the flower that was pinned to her shirt and then quietly walked away with it.

Tippy And Toffee

We got Carsten and Willy each a new kitten to play with. Carsten's kitten was a little black one with a white tip on the end of his tail and he named it "Tippy". Willy's was a little toffee coloured one so he called it Toffee.

Carsten's kitten ended up getting sick and dying. We went and got Carsten a new kitten. But the new kitten we got was orange and Carsten didn't want an orange kitten; he wanted a black kitten. So even though we said things to Carsten like "Aww, the kitten is so sad that you don't want to play with him" Carsten did not want to have anything to do with him. Then one day, we were cleaning the stove pipes for the wood stove and the new kitten ran right through them getting himself all black and sooty. I said to Carsten "Look! The kitten is so sad that you don't want him that he has tried to make himself black like your last kitten so that you will love him". And that did it. Ever since then Carsten took to the kitten and began to love him.

Josephine And The Wild Cat

Willy's kitten grew up and eventually became blind. When we opened the door to let her out she would often miss the opening and hit her head against the wall with a resounding 'thud'. When she finally died, Willy got another kitten from his friend, Jack Oliver. It was a long haired black female with a bit of white on it. The chin was white on one side and black on the other side. Willy called her Josephine.

One cold winter day a wild bob cat came into the barn looking to make a meal out of Josephine's kittens. Josephine was much smaller than the bob cat but when it came to defending her kittens she was as fierce as any wild cat. She ran after that bob cat with a scream and with claws out. There was a loud noisy battle between the two cats.

The fight carried on into the pen where the Jersey bull was tied. While the cats were rolling in a screaming cat fight right under the bull, the bull was bucking as if he was in a rodeo with a rider on him. The noise attracted Rex. He was outside and wanted to get into the barn. I opened the door and Josephine chased that bob cat outside where Rex killed it.

Wally

One of Josephine's kittens was a beige cat which Willy loved so much he took it into the house. One day Willy's kitten somehow managed to crawl through a hole in the wall and refused to come out. He was a bit scared and felt safer living in the wall. We would put food just outside the hole in hopes of coaxing him out but as soon as he saw us he would run back inside the wall. This led to us naming him "Wally.

Newt In The Sink

There was no running water on the farm like you get from the faucet now a days. Instead the rain water went into a rain barrel outside and that was hooked up to a pump faucet in the kitchen inside. Every time you wanted some water in the sink you had to pump the handle and the water would come out.

One summer morning, Carsten was pumping the water into the sink to wash his hands when all of a sudden "Ploop!" Out plopped a little newt. Carsten said "Well hello there!" and he picked it up and took it out side and put it into the rain barrel.

The next morning Carsten once again was pumping water to wash his hands and once again the little newt plopped into the sink. "Hello again!" Carsten said and once again took the newt back out to the rain barrel. This happened every morning for the whole summer.

Carsten and a container full of baby chicks

Hatching Chicks

Occasionally things do not always go as planned on a farm and you have to think fast and make do with what you've got. One day one of the hens, who was just about to hatch her chicks, died. There were not many other options because there were no other available hens at the time and no warming lamps either. The eggs couldn't be allowed to get cold so we had to think of something fast. Carsten and Willy would take turns doing certain chores. On this particular day Willy had gotten up early to do the chores and it was Carsten's turn to sleep in a little. I quickly scooped up all the eggs and took them into the house where Carsten was still sleeping. I put the eggs into the bed with him to keep warm and one by one the eggs hatched. Soon Carsten was a new mom to a bunch of baby chicks!

John And The Skates

While we lived at the farm Carsten and Willy made new friends. One of them was named John. John's family were very strict religious people and on Sundays after church they were not allowed to do many things. In the winter, all the other kids in the

64

neighbourhood would go down to the frozen lake after church and go ice skating. But this was one thing that John was not allowed to do on a Sunday.

His sisters would pass him his skates through a basement window. Then he would leave and meet his friends down at the lake. The lake was on our farm. One day John fell through the ice while skating with Carsten and Willy. He went back to our farm and dried all his clothes out before heading back home. John stayed as a life long friend of Carsten and Willy. He came very often to our home on Sundays where he was able to disobey his father, the Free Methodist Minister, by playing with Carsten and Willy and having a good time.

11. HERE WE ARE

The sign they found in the school-house the day they first arrived

Ivan's Ham Radio

A letter (or speech) from Vera to an unknown group of people

Ivan had several heart attacks. They began in 1963 and got worse each time. He had to work less and take lots of medication. He was in and out of the hospital for years. I did lots of the work for him. But in 1966 at Christmas I had a breast cancer operation.

We finally sold the farm in October of 1967. Ivan was only 55 and couldn't get a pension yet. So he grabbed a job as a caretaker in the Campbellford High School. We also bought "The Little Red School-House" where I am still living.

When Ivan worked in the Campbellford High School he met the electronics teacher, Dick Maki. He got Ivan interested in Ham radio. That was a blessing for Ivan. He spent all his retirement years on the radio and met lots of other Hams all over the world.

I remember the first time he had contacted a Danish Ham operator. Dick Maki called VE3-KFD (Ivan's radio call letters).

Ivan on his Ham radio

Ivan rushed to the radio. Dick said "Ivan, I have a Dane on my radio. I will let you two talk to each other." That Dane was Henning Floor. Ivan was very excited. From then on he met all the nice Danes. It became part of his life. Thank you all!

Ivan retired in August of 1977 and started to become a Ham radio operator full time.

Out Into The World

Carsten and Willy eventually grew up and moved away from home. Carsten became a fisheries biologist, married his wife Brenda and had three daughters, Dana, Heather and Anika and a son who was also named Carsten. Willy became a life guard at Wassaga Beach as well as a Folk singer. Willy married his wife Donna and had a daughter named Polly. But even though they grew up and moved out, they always came back to visit at the Little Red School-House year after year and now they brought their children with them.

Farfar's World

In the words of Vera as told to her granddaughter Dana

Farfar had a little room in the school-house that was his radio room. On the wall was a map of the world with coloured pins all over it indicating all the places he had spoken to someone over the Ham radio. When you were two, Dana, you came with your parents for a visit. In the afternoon we put you down for a nap on the little fold up bed that is in the radio room. But instead of napping you took an interest in Farfar's map. He also had a plastic inflatable globe sitting on his desk. You decided to climb up onto the desk and you took the pins out of the map and started to stick them into the inflatable globe just like Farfar did with his map. Of course the globe started to lose air and began to shrivel up. As you watched the globe collapse you started to cry. We all came rushing in to see what was the matter and you said "I broke Farfar's world! I broke Farfar's world!"

The Skunk In The T.V. Tower

When you look out the huge windows of the school-house you can see a very tall metal tower hugging the side of the outside wall. This tall metal tower is how the signal gets to the T.V. for the 3 or 4 available stations in the area. When you were two or three years old you were sitting on the couch watching T.V. when all of a sudden you jumped up and excitedly pointed at the window saying "Look! There is a skunk in the T.V. tower!" Everyone rushed to the window expecting to see a skunk climbing the tower and were wondering what they were going to do about it. But when they looked outside they all had a good laugh because the skunk turned out to be nothing more than a black squirrel.

Popping grapes

In the words of Vera as told to her family

One morning when Dana was two she woke up earlier than everyone else and went out to play in the living room. I awoke to the sound of a faint little "pop, pop, pop" sound. Curious as to what the sound was I looked out my bedroom door and found Dana sitting by the coffee table. She was pulling off all the red plastic grapes that I had as a decoration in a red glass cornicopia on the table. One by one she pulled the off with a little "pop" sound each time. I watched her for a few moments until finally she realized that I was there. With a look of surprise and worry she started to gather all the popped grapes up and said " I will throw them in the garbage, Farmor. I will throw them in the garbage."

Ivan in the West Edmonton Mall in Alberta, Canada

Farfar's Beeping
One evening I asked Carsten Andrew (Vera's grandson), who was only two at the time, to go and get his Farfar to come to the supper table. Carsten went to one of the rooms to find him but came back shortly saying "Farfar's beeping! Farfar's beeping!" We thought that maybe he meant that Farfar was on his ham radio and using the beeping noises of morse code or something to talk to people over the radio. But what he had really been trying to tell us was that "Farfar was sleeping".

69

Vera and Polly

Polly

When Willy and his wife were going through a divorce, Vera's grand daughter, Polly, went to stay with her and Ivan for awhile. Vera and Ivan had a wonderful time with Polly and enjoyed taking her places and doing things with her. Vera taught Polly how to knit little rabbits that Polly gave to each of her family members. They would go camping and play games and tell stories. Vera had only ever had boys around the house so she was thrilled that she was able to spend some girl time with her oldest grand daughter.

Polly

In the words of Polly as told to Dana

I was always afraid of the ghost stories that Farmor told me. One day I had to ride my bike down to visit a friend on the farm that was down the road and up another lane that lay between dense forest edges. I stayed a little too long and had to ride home in the dusk instead of in the daylight. As I rode I felt uneasy about the forest looking black and dark on both sides of me. Suddenly a big white ghost drifted out of the woods and straight down the lane at me! Then it swooped and turned around and came at me again! I peddled faster than I ever did before to get back to the school-house. When I got there I asked if we could ring the bell to scare away the spirit for fear that it had followed me home.

In the end it turned out that the big white ghost was only just a big white owl.

Bats In The Belfry

The back of the Little Red School-House has an old closed off chimney that isn't used anymore. Inside lives a colony of bats. Every evening at dusk you can go and stand in the back yard and look way up to the top of the chimney where the tip of the roof meets at a point. If you stand watching long enough you can see the bats start to squeeze out of the tiny hole and fly off for the night to catch mosquitoes and other bugs. This was an evening ritual for the grand kids when they came to visit in the summer.

One evening Dana, Heather and Vera were all looking up, intent on the emerging bats, when to the right and out of the corner of our eye we saw the largest bat we had ever seen in our lives! It was about three feet tall and had about a 5 foot wingspan and it lifted off the ground and flew over our heads almost hitting us!

Or so we thought. As it turns out the giant bat was not a bat at all but instead was an owl that had been near by and since we had been standing so quietly to watch the bats it wasn't bothered by us until we moved just a little and started talking to each other. Then it got scared and flew off leaving us to our wild imagination of giant bats.

12. MUSIC, DOGS AND EUCHRE

Ivan had suffered multiple heart attacks over the years and hadn't been expected to live more than a few years. But he beat the odds and lived almost 20 more years. Finally his heart gave out on September 29th, 1985 in the little town of Campbellford, Ontario at the age of seventy three.

I was now all alone in the Little Red School-House. My kids and grand children came to visit me once in awhile but they lived far away and it just wasn't the same.

I had the neighbours Bob and Bill Scott in the next farm over who would stop by and take care of things around the house for me, like mowing the lawn and fixing the fence. I used to take care of their mom and do some house work for her many years ago. Now they are always looking out for me.

I spent much of my time gardening and caring for my flowers. And I would go to church every Sunday which was a good way to socialize with other people and to get out of the house for a bit.

I always said that I was too old to marry again and could not see myself with anyone other than Ivan. So I decided that I would just live alone for the rest of my days in my Little Red School-House. Then one spring day in 1987 along came Henry and changed all that.

Vera and Henry

73

Henry

In the words of Vera in a phone call to her granddaughter Dana

"I wanted to ask you if you would be all right with you if I got married again. I know it seems fast and that it wasn't long ago that your Farfar died but I have met a man from church named Henry and he has asked me to marry him. Before I say yes to him I want to make sure that the family is all right with this.

Let me tell you how I met him. You see, Henry is a Dutchman that came to Canada from Holland many years ago. He lost his wife a few years back and he has been lonely. He prayed to God to find him a wife and he had a list of things that he was looking for. He was looking for a lady that believes in God, preferably an immigrant from Europe and that she must love dogs because he is a dog trainer. So he went to Pastor Pye and asked if he knew of anyone who fit the bill. Pastor Pye thought of me and introduced him one day after the church service. I did not know that Henry was looking for a wife and I just thought he was a nice man and I shook his hand and we talked for a bit about dogs and music. I thought nothing more of it and went back home.

A few days later I heard a knock at my door and I was surprised to see that there was Henry standing outside on my door step. He had asked the ladies at the church where I lived and then popped by for a visit. We stood outside talking for a bit about music and I mention that I had an organ in the living room that hadn't been played in a few years because it used to be your Farfar's and I do not know how to play it. His eyes lit right up and he asked if he could come in and play some songs on it. So I invited him in for coffee. He sat down at the organ and played some hymns that he knew and the two of us sang and had a great time.

He left a few hours later and asked if he might visit me again the next week. So for the past few months he has been coming by to visit and drink coffee and to play songs on the organ. Then the other day he asked me to marry him. I never thought that I would ever get married again but if the family is all right with it then I would like to say yes."

Farmor and Opa taking a walk down Goacher Road

The entire family was happy that Vera had found someone to make her happy and they all gave her their blessing. Vera and Henry were married in the summer of 1987 and Henry was officially welcomed into the family and the grand children called him "Opa" (Dutch for grandfather).

Opa brought with him a renewed sense of child like fun to their marriage. They bought a boat and often packed a lunch and went for an afternoon boat ride. She would entertain the family with stories of their adventures everytime the family came to visit.

In the words of Vera as told to Dana

" The other day Opa and I took the boat out on the Trent river. We packed a picnic lunch and stayed out all day. We would pretend that we were river pirates and whenever we saw another boat coming our way we would say to each other 'Avast! Get out the cannons! Shoot when you see the whites of their eyes! Don't let them board us!' Once the other boats got close enough to hear us we would suddenly go quiet and just smile and wave as they passed by. Then when they were out of ear shot again we would say 'Those scally-wags! Look at 'em go! Arggh!"

Opa and the grandchildren riding the ATV

Opa also bought a four wheeler that he used for gathering fire wood and traveling around in the woods with. The grandkids were always excited when Opa offered to take them for a ride down the road on the ATV. With the wind in their hair and the squeals of delight they zipped up and down the lane and through the big yard. Sometimes we wondered who was having more fun, the grand kids or Opa.

One thing the two of them shared was a love of dogs. Opa was an obedience dog trainer and had won many medals for his dogs. To Farmor's delight it wasn't long before they owned, not one dog, but two! They had a German Shepherd named Smokey and a Golden Retriever named Sandy. They took those two dogs with them everywhere they went and the dogs won many medals in the numerous dog shows that they entered.

Opa with Smokey and Sandy

Aside form dog shows, they also started to go weekly to the local Euchre tournaments at the community centre. Opa fancied himself to be a master Euchre player and would challenge anyone to a game. He especially liked to play when the family came o visit. The games were always Good Guys vs. Bad Guys.

The Good Guys vs The Bad Guys

If you were on his team then you were one of the "Good Guys" and if you played against him then you were one of the "Bad Guys".

Vera and Henry had many adventures and fun until Opa's health started to fail. Then the next few years for Vera were hard on her as she spent tireless hours looking after Henry and nursing him through the different stages of the kidney disease that he suffered from. Finally on March 30, 1999 Henry passed away. Vera was all alone once again in the Little Red School-House with only the company of her dog Sandy (Smokey had passed away a few years previous).

As time went on Vera developed glaucoma and she could no longer see very well. She had to wear sunglasses to go outside because the sun hurt her eyes and she had to put drops in her eyes every day. When you can't see very well it can make things difficult in your day to day life.

Rice Pudding

One year Dana and Riley went to visit Vera for Christmas. Now, in Denmark it is tradition at Christmas time to make a rice pudding. Hidden inside one of the bowls of rice pudding is an almond. Whoever gets the almond gets a present. Once the grandchildren came along, the family changed the tradition a little bit and they put an almond in everyone's bowl and everyone got a present (this was so that the kids didn't cry and argue over who got the present). So on this particular Christmas Vera brought out the bowls of rice pudding and we all eagerly dug into the pudding and started eating. You can imagine our surprise when we went to eat the almonds and they tasted horrible! "What is this?" Vera cried out. Dana who hadn't eaten her almond yet, wiped away the rice pudding that was covering it and took a closer look. They weren't almonds at all! "These are uncooked lima beans!" Dana exclaimed. Vera started laughing and laughing. Soon we were all laughing. Vera had a little jar of lima beans in he cupboard and had mistakenly thought they were almonds. After all, they were about the right shape and size. She never forgot it. It became an inside joke and every year at Christmas time she would ask us "Did you find your lima bean in your rice pudding?"

Once Henry had passed on, Vera became more involved with her community and joined the local book club called the "Goacher Girls" (Goacher was the name of the road that most of them lived on). These ladies would get together for coffee on a regular basis to read and discuss books. However, since Vera's eye sight was so bad and she was not able to read the books, the Goacher Girls would have her tell them one of her own personal stories instead. It was one way that the community could include her. Another thing they would do together in the community was the annual spring garbage pick up. Vera was happy to make the newspaper about it one year.

CAMPBELLFORD EDITION

Goacher Road volunteers complete spring clean-up

Senior citizen Vera Goeree, 89, didn't allow her age to get in the way as she took part as a volunteer with the Goacher Road Clean-Up crew. She was among the group of 30 volunteers who pitched in to make sure their community in the Meyersburg vicinity looked spruced up with spring finally making an appearance once again. Photo: Rob De Lint.

Organized again by Dave Burnham, the second annual Goacher Road Spring Clean-Up went off successfully. Almost 30 men, women and children clad in orange safety vests cleaned roadsides and ditches on Beaver Road, Goacher Road from County Road 30 to Mahoney Road, as well as Dump Road from Mahoney Road to Bannon, and Bannon Road all the way to the Hastings Road.

As one of the cleaners noted, it is disturbing that this type of effort should even be necessary.

"If trucks tarped their loads, much of the litter would not blow off. Of course it is almost impossible to legislate against the picnic people enjoying the relative peace and quiet of the sideroads, sipping Tim Hortons' coffee, then pitching out the cups, followed by food containers," he commented.

The bagged litter and refuse filled four pick-up trucks. Tires, a fridge, a television set, a coffee table and assorted chairs, fencing and swimming pool skimmer, hoses and tarps made up some of the loads. More than 40 garbage bags were filled.

The group started the cleanup at 9:30 a.m and finished before 1 p.m

This year the ranks almost doubled in size. Ages of the volunteers included 89-year-old Vera Goeree all the way to the McFadyen brothers, Isaac, and 18-month-old Gabriel. This year's potluck dinner featured two birthday cakes, Isaac celebrating his third birthday and George Scott getting an early start on his 70th.

The Goacher Road Clean-up crew thanks Trent Hills for supplying the garbage bags and gloves and disposing of the accumulated garbage.

Vera in the Campbellford newspaper – April 2007

In September of 2010 she was asked to do the survivors lap for the Campbellford's Relay For Life walk for cancer. She was tickled pink by this and felt like a celebrity. After all, she had survived three different types of cancer throughout her life time.

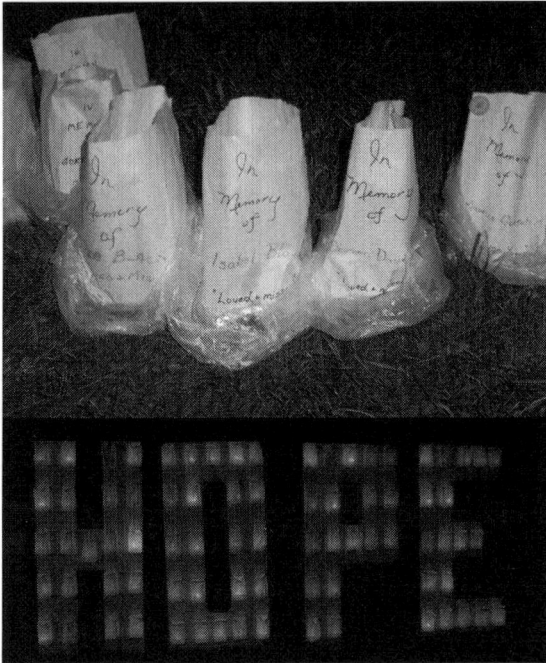

Candles in paper bags
in memory of loved ones lost.
Campbellford's Relay For Life - September 10, 2010

13. GREAT GRANDCHILDREN

Now more than ever, Vera enjoyed the visits from her family and from the great-grand kids in particular because she never lost her sense of child like humour and fun.

Dylan

It was Mother's Day and Farmor was coming to North Bay for a visit. Heather had bought a box of candies as a present for her but Dylan kept wanting to eat them. Finally, in an effort to get Dylan to stop trying to eat the candies, Heather told him "They are yuckie and will make you sick". That did the trick and he stopped trying to eat them. So a few hours later when Vera arrived Dylan greeted her and handed her the present saying "Here is a present for you!....They are yuckie and will make you sick!" - age 4

Riley

While visiting Farmor one summer we all took a trip to Pres'quile Provincial Park. We went for a walk down by the light house. After awhile Farmor asked Riley "Where is your mom?" To which she replied "Oh she is over there with the red hair. If you see anyone with red hair it's most likely my mom." - age 5

One of our favourite games to play while visiting Farmor was Chinese Checkers. Farmor asked Riley if I wanted to play. So Riley turned to me and asked "Mommy, do you want to play 'Tiny Stickers" with me and Farmor?" - age 5

We had gone to Farmor's house for Thanksgiving. After the turkey dinner there was pumpkin pie for dessert. Riley asked Farmor " Can I have some of that Punky Pie?"
- age 6

I had bought Riley some play money from the toy store before going on a visit to Farmor at the Little Red School-House. While she was there she asked Farmor to play hospital with her. Farmor lay on the sofa and pretended to be sick. The first thing Riley did was to hand Farmor a cheque and ask "Do you know how long you will be staying?" - age 6

While playing hospital Riley told Farmor " Here is enough medicine for the rest of your life....101 days." - age 6

Riley was drinking a glass of chocolate milk when Farmor came along and took a sip. Riley gasped and said "Don't you know you could get my germs?!" Then she paused for a moment and said "But that's OK. You won't get them because you didn't drink all of it." - age 6

We were visiting Farmor for Christmas and having Christmas dinner. Each of us were sitting in the seats we usually sit in when we come to dinner. Riley leaned over and whispered to Farmor "When we go all these seats will be yours!" - age 6

We went to visit Farmor for the March Break . One evening I took Farmor's dog, Sandy, out for a walk. I was gone for quite a long time. Riley started to get anxious and asked Farmor "Where did my mommy go? What is taking her so long?" Jokingly, Farmor said " Maybe she won't come back. Maybe she got tired of you and left you here with me." Riley thought for a moment and then said "She always was tired of me, but she never gave me away before." - age 6

Farmor's dog, Sandy, had gotten too old and sick so he had to be put down. Riley had known this dog all her life and was very fond of him. When she was told that Sandy had died she said "I guess Farmor will only have Balto for comfort when we visit her". (Balto was Riley's dog) - age 8

Devin
We had gone to visit Farmor one day. When it was time to say 'good bye' grandma said to Devin "Go inside and say good-bye and thank you for everything". So Devin went inside and said to Farmor "Good bye! And thank you!" When Farmor asked him "Thank you for what?" Devin replied "For something." - age 4

Sam

After her dog, Sandy, had passed away Vera had decided that she was too old to have another dog. She was afraid that any dog she got would out live her and she did not want to worry about what would happen to the dog once she was gone. So although it broke her heart not to have a dog around, she chose to do what she felt was best.

Her neighbours, Marion and Robert De Lint ran a bed and breakfast just down the road from Vera. They had a little cocker spaniel dog named Sam. Sam loved people and was often found hanging around the guests looking for table scraps. One day the De Lints had to go away for a few days so they asked Vera to look after Sam for them while they were gone. Vera, who missed having a dog, readily agreed to this. Sam also liked Vera's company and the two became close pals.

Over time the De Lints asked Vera to look after their dog, Sam, more and more often until one day the De Lints did not come to pick up Sam on the day that they had said they would. Instead, a few days later, Robert came to Vera's door and said that he had spoken to his wife and they had a proposal to make. They wanted to know if Sam could stay with her indefinitely. They would pay for Sam's food and vet bills and they would still own the dog, but the dog would live with her. They explained that with all the guests they had at their bed and breakfast they did not always have time to spend with Sam. And besides, he was getting fat from all the table scraps that all the guests were giving him. By this time Vera had fallen in love with Sam and although she was a bit hesitant she agreed to take Sam in on a more permanent basis. And so it was through this selfless act of the De Lint's that Vera was able to have a dog again and Sam could have the love and attention of two families.

Corbin, Willy, Vera, Polly, Chloe

Willy lived on the other side of the country in Alberta and was not able to spend the time he wished he could with her. Polly lived in the U.S.A in Nebraska with her family. She too wished that she was able to visit more often. So one day they planned a special trip to go together as a family to visit Vera. Willy, Polly, her husband Bruce and their children Corbin and Chloe flew hundreds of miles to reunite at the Little Red School-House. Vera was able to meet her great-grand children for the first time and she was thrilled about it. While they visited they had a fantastic time catching up and playing games and having fun.

During the last few months of her life Vera began to suffer from dementia and did not always recognize her family members. Her sight had begun to fail her years before and she could no longer drive. There came a point where her son Carsten and his wife Brenda moved in with her so that she did not have to leave her Little Red School-House and go to an old age home.

Most days were spent playing Yahtzee over and over again until no one ever wanted to see a Yahtzee game again. But they kept playing it anyways because it was one of the only games left that she was able to play and because they loved her.

This time was trying and at times difficult for the people she loved because it hurts your heart when someone you love no longer recognizes you or when they think they are still living in the past. But there were still many joyful days and sometimes even humourous ones.

You run a wonderful establishment here

The Christmas of 2010 Carsten and Brenda brought Vera to North Bay to have a visit with the grandchildren and great grandchildren. Since she was not in her usual and familiar surroundings she did not comprehend exactly where she was. From the moment she arrived she was doted on and was given good food and her favourite desserts. She had a full and busy day and she was very happy. When it was time for bed she was shown the room that she was to sleep in. As she went into the bedroom and was about to shut the door she turned around and said. "This has been so nice! You people run a wonderful establishment here!" We all had a great chuckle because we were pretty certain she thought she was staying in a motel.

14. RINGING OF THE BELL

In the words of Vera as told to Dana

"When I die, don't cry. Be happy because I believe in God and I will be in heaven. Besides, I can't see well anymore and I can't hear well anymore so it is hard to do things. I am happy and I am ready to go."

The bell on top of the school-house

Vera died peacefully on April 27th, 2011 at the age of ninety three. After the memorial service, people from all over gathered at the Little Red School-House for a BBQ in her honour.

Not only did all of her family attend, but so did the Goacher Girls, the neighbours and some long time friends. They celebrated her life and told her stories and shared the memories that each person had. They remembered her the way she wanted to be remembered. And as an added tribute, each one of those who were there took a turn pulling on the rope and ringing the school bell one last time.

The bell rang out long and loud throughout the country side. It didn't stop ringing until the line up of people had each had their turn to ring out their rememberance of her. And as the last tones of the bell faded on the wind there was a heaviness of hearts as we knew that would be the last time we would hear that bell ring. It was the last time because we had to sell that Little Red School-

House. Soon it would belong to someone else and we would no longer be able to enter inside. Another family would start their stories here and hopefully love this place as much as we did. Even if we could have kept the Little Red School-House, it wouldn't have been the same without our Farmor living in it.

The Little Red School-House as it looked in 2015

In the words of Dana as told to you

In September of 2015, just over 4 years later, my brother, Carsten, his girlfriend and I stop in Campbellford on our way back from a camping trip. We decided to swing by the old school-house to see what it looked like now. The stop was an emotional one for my brother and I. We almost didn't stop at all, but we wanted to see the Little Red School-House that our Farmor had lived in before she passed away. We hadn't seen it since the new owners moved in. So although we wanted to see it; at the same time we were worried that we would be heart broken by any changes that we saw.

We pulled up near the mailboxes and made ourselves look like lost tourists as best we could. There was a lady in a blue shirt working in the flower garden at the side of the house. The old dog house was gone but there were two beautiful dogs playing in the yard. Farmor would have been happy about that. She adored dogs, and she adored her flowers. Not much else had changed. The original door was replaced by a new one and the side of the garage was now blue instead of white. Our favourite tree had been cut down, but it had been in bad shape and really did need to come down anyways. In it's place they had planted a brand new sapling that, in time, I am sure will become a beautiful big tree. We only stayed for a very short moment or two. Just long enough to get a glimpse and take a quick picture through the windshield of the car. We didn't want to look like stalkers so we quickly moved on. I left feeling happy that the the people living there now seemed to be happy and taking great care of the place. It was a bitter sweet moment.

Just as every story has a beginning, it also has an end. Or does it? Our stories continue on as our family continues on. We may not have the Little Red School-House anymore but we still have our family and we are still creating and living out new stories day by day.

ABOUT THE AUTHOR

Dana Woodard was born and raised in North Bay, Ontario, Canada.

She didn't grow up intending to write any books. In fact she just wanted to do her crafts, read her books, and play her video games.

Both as a child and as an adult she had heard the stories her Farmor had told her about the war and about living on the farm and she knew that once Farmor had passed on there was a danger of those stories being lost. Some family members had tape recorded some of the stories and others had written some down. But Dana wanted to bring all those stories together in one place that her family could share.

She plans to write at least two more books in The Little Red School-House series. You can look for more on those titles and read more about Dana Woodard and other books that she has published by following her author profile on Good Reads at: www.goodreads.com/author/show/9864884.Dana_Woodard

47268767R00053

Made in the USA
San Bernardino, CA
27 March 2017